D1465856

THE AMERICAN SADDLEBRED HORSE

By Rachel Grack

Consultant:
Dr. Emily Leuthner
DVM, MS, DACVIM
Country View Veterinary Service
Oregon, Wisc.

BELLWETHER MEDIA • MINNEAPOLIS, MN

Jump into the cockpit and take flight with Pilot Books. Your journey will take you on high-energy adventures as you learn about all that is wild, weird, fascinating, and fun!

This edition first published in 2012 by Bellwether Media, Inc.

No part of this publication may be reproduced in whole or in part without written permission of the publisher. For information regarding permission, write to Bellwether Media, Inc., Attention: Permissions Department, 5357 Penn Avenue South, Minneapolis, MN 55419.

Library of Congress Cataloging-in-Publication Data

Koestler-Grack, Rachel A., 1973-
The American saddlebred horse / by Rachel Grack.
   p. cm. – (Pilot books. Horse breed roundup)
Includes bibliographical references and index.
 Summary: "Engaging images accompany information about the American Saddlebred Horse. The combination of high-interest subject matter and narrative text is intended for students in grades 3 through 7"–Provided by publisher.
ISBN 978-1-60014-654-1 (hardcover : alk. paper)
 1. American saddlebred horse–Juvenile literature. I. Title.
SF293.A5K64 2012
636.1'3–dc22   2011010412

Printed in the United States of America, North Mankato, MN.

080111   1187

CONTENTS

The American Saddlebred Horse

The crowd watches a graceful American Saddlebred **trot** and **canter** around the **show ring**. Judges pay close attention to how the horse performs these **gaits**. When the horse finishes, the judges give it high scores and the crowd applauds with delight. The American Saddlebred has won the competition!

The American Saddlebred Horse is often called "the American Horse" because the breed was developed in the United States. Farmers wanted to breed a great working and riding horse. They used the Narragansett Pacer, the Thoroughbred, and other breeds to produce the American Saddlebred. The breed gained the **endurance** and smooth gait of Narragansett Pacers. It also inherited the long legs of Thoroughbreds.

The Original American Horse

The Narragansett Pacer was the first horse breed developed in the United States. Sadly, it is now extinct.

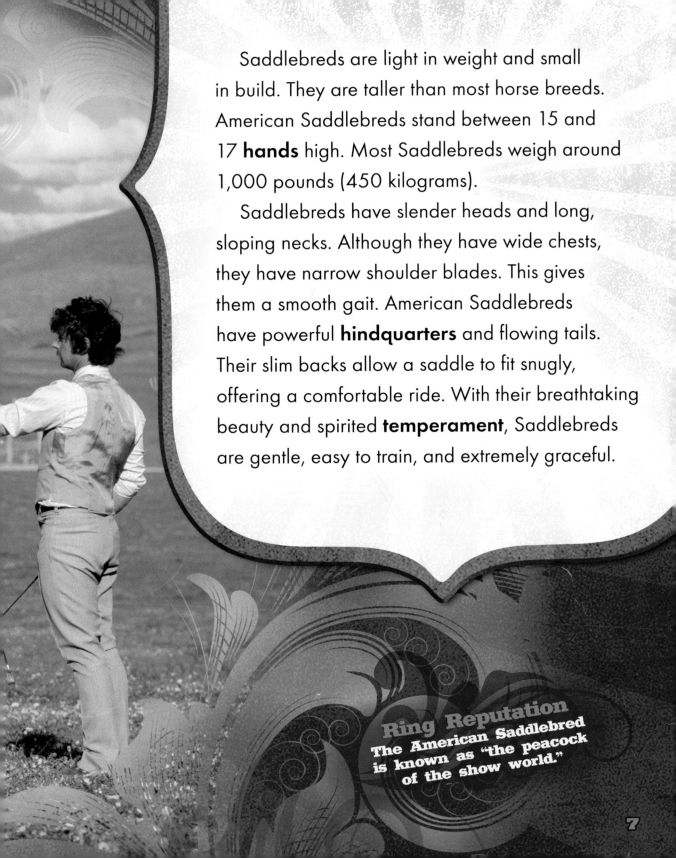

Saddlebreds are light in weight and small in build. They are taller than most horse breeds. American Saddlebreds stand between 15 and 17 **hands** high. Most Saddlebreds weigh around 1,000 pounds (450 kilograms).

Saddlebreds have slender heads and long, sloping necks. Although they have wide chests, they have narrow shoulder blades. This gives them a smooth gait. American Saddlebreds have powerful **hindquarters** and flowing tails. Their slim backs allow a saddle to fit snugly, offering a comfortable ride. With their breathtaking beauty and spirited **temperament**, Saddlebreds are gentle, easy to train, and extremely graceful.

Ring Reputation
The American Saddlebred is known as "the peacock of the show world."

All-American History

In the 1600s, colonists brought Galloway and Hobbie horses with them to North America from Europe. These horses were small and sturdy. They were easy and comfortable to ride for long distances over rugged terrain. When the colonists **crossbred** these two horses, the result was the Narragansett Pacer. The name came from Narragansett Bay, Rhode Island, where the first of the breed was born. In the 1700s, the Narragansett Pacer was bred with the Thoroughbred. Morgans, Arabians, Standardbreds, and other breeds also contributed to the **bloodline**. The result was the American Horse.

A Historical Ride

Many historians believe American colonist Paul Revere took his famous "Midnight Ride" on the back of a Narragansett Pacer.

Paul Revere

Kentucky is called "horse country" and is often referred to as the birthplace of the modern American Saddlebred.

As Americans moved west in the early 1800s, many of these horses ended up in Kentucky. There, people kept breeding the American Horse with the Thoroughbred. This produced a larger horse with a very smooth gait. People called this horse a Kentucky Saddler. As the Western **frontier** grew, **pioneers** took these horses into Ohio, Tennessee, and Missouri.

Many military officers rode Kentucky Saddlers during the **American Civil War**. Union General Ulysses S. Grant rode one named Cincinnati, and Confederate General Robert E. Lee rode one named Traveller. After the war, Kentucky Saddlers stood out in horse shows, impressing people with their beauty and grace. Eventually, they became known as American Saddlebreds. In 1891, the American Saddlebred Horse Association (ASHA) formed in Louisville, Kentucky.

Robert E. Lee

Ulysses S. Grant

Inside and Outside the Show Ring

Elegant and graceful, American Saddlebreds make excellent show horses. In the show ring, horses are judged on their gaits. American Saddlebreds are built to perform five different gaits. Each gait contains a certain number of **beats**. A beat occurs each time the horse's hooves hit the ground. The **walk**, trot, and canter are gaits that come naturally to all horses. The American Saddlebred can also learn the **slow gait** and the **rack**.

Bouncy Step

For competitions, a Saddlebred's hooves are grown extra long and fitted with heavy shoes. This gives them a bouncy step.

The walk is a slow and springy gait in which the horse moves one hoof at a time. It lifts its left front hoof, right back hoof, right front hoof, and lastly, left back hoof. This is a four-beat gait.

The trot is a faster, two-beat gait. In a trot, the horse lifts two hooves that are diagonal from each other at the same time. For example, the horse lifts its right front hoof and its left back hoof together. Then it lifts the next pair before the first pair touches the ground. For a split second, it looks like the horse is floating in midair!

The canter is a three-beat gait. The horse pushes off with one back hoof. Then the other back hoof and opposite front hoof hit the ground to create the second beat. The final beat occurs when the opposite front hoof touches the ground. Like the trot, the canter has a moment when the horse appears to be floating.

Training Saddlebreds to perform the slow gait and the rack takes time, patience, and a great deal of knowledge. In both of these gaits, each hoof hits the ground in a separate beat. The slow gait is precise and controlled. The rack is a fast and flashy version of the slow gait. This gait creates a very smooth ride. People love watching Saddlebreds perform the slow gait and the rack in the show ring!

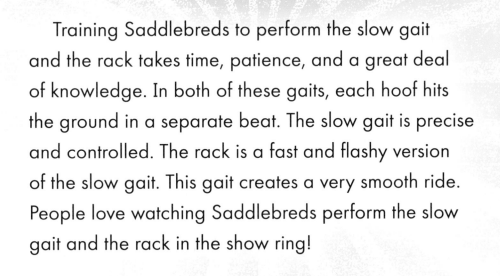

Tom Bass

Tom Bass was a famous horse trainer. He worked with many Saddlebreds, especially those with difficult temperaments. Bass was a gentle trainer. Instead of disciplining a horse, he would talk to it and develop a relationship with it. His horses won many championships, and his success allowed him to meet five U.S. presidents.

Famous American Saddlebreds

Denmark

Denmark began the Denmark family of American Saddlebreds in 1839. For 150 years, the Denmark bloodline was the most respected Saddlebred family. Today, many American Saddlebreds can be traced back to Denmark.

Harrison Chief

Harrison Chief was another important American Saddlebred. He was a descendent of Messenger, a Thoroughbred that was brought to the United States in 1788. Messenger was a foundation horse of the Standardbred Horse breed. In the 1800s, the Denmark and Chief horse families crossed bloodlines. As soon as these two horse families mixed, the American Saddlebred became a major horse breed.

Rex McDonald

In the late 1800s, a black American Saddlebred named Rex McDonald stole the hearts of American horse lovers. Rex McDonald was defeated only three times throughout his entire career in the show ring. Many U.S. presidents traveled to St. Louis, Missouri to meet him.

Although Saddlebreds are most famous for their abilities in the show ring, they also excel in other areas. Friendly, smart, and fast, Saddlebreds are suited for almost any activity. Many people enjoy using them for trail riding, and others use them for ranch work.

Today, the ASHA has **registered** more than 250,000 Saddlebreds. The breed is most common in Kentucky, Ohio, Tennessee, Virginia, and Pennsylvania. However, Saddlebreds can be found in every state, as well as in Canada, Europe, Australia, and Japan. The American Saddlebred is one of the most admired horse breeds in the world. Many people call Saddlebreds "a jewel of a breed," one with extraordinary beauty and class.

Glossary

American Civil War—a war fought between the Northern states and the Southern states of the U.S. from 1861 to 1865

beats—steps in a gait; a beat can be made by one hoof at a time or two hooves together.

bloodline—the family history of a horse

canter—a quick, three-beat natural gait

crossbred—used two different horse breeds to produce a new kind of horse

endurance—the ability to do something for a long time

frontier—unexplored wilderness on the edge of settled land; the West was the great frontier of the United States in the 1800s.

gaits—the ways in which a horse moves; walking, trotting, and cantering are examples of gaits.

hands—the units used to measure the height of a horse; one hand is equal to 4 inches (10.2 centimeters).

hindquarters—the back legs and muscles of a four-legged animal

pioneers—the first people to settle a new territory

rack—a four-beat gait performed at the speed of a trot or faster

registered—made record of; owners register their horses with official breed organizations.

show ring—the ring where horses compete and are displayed at a horse show

slow gait—a four-beat gait performed at a slower speed than the rack

temperament—personality or nature; the American Saddlebred has a spirited temperament.

trot—a two-beat natural gait that can be fast or slow

walk—the slowest gait of a horse

To Learn More

At the Library

Coleman, Lori. *The American Saddlebred Horse.*
Mankato, Minn.: Capstone Press, 2006.

Gentle, Victor, and Janet Perry. *Saddlebreds.* Milwaukee,
Wisc.: Gareth Stevens Pub., 2001.

Goldish, Meish. *Hollywood Horses.* New York, N.Y.:
Bearport Pub., 2008.

On the Web

Learning more about American Saddlebreds
is as easy as 1, 2, 3.

1. Go to www.factsurfer.com.

2. Enter "American Saddlebreds" into the search box.

3. Click the "Surf" button and you will see a list of
related Web sites.

With factsurfer.com, finding more information
is just a click away.

Index

The images in this book are reproduced through the courtesy of: blickwinkel / Alamy, front cover; Wildlife GmbH / Alamy, pp. 4-5, 8-9, 12-13; Jean Paul Ferrero / ardea.com, pp. 6-7; Time & Life Pictures / Getty Images, p. 8 (small); Jeff Banke, pp. 10, 14-15; Mary Evans Picture Library / Alamy, p. 11 (left); North Wind Picture Archives / Alamy, p. 11 (right); Juniors Bildarchiv / Age Fotostock, pp. 16-17; The State Historical Society of Missouri, p. 17 (small); Juniors Bildarchiv / Photolibrary, pp. 18-19; Sabine Stuewer / KimballStock, pp. 20-21.

42/15

For Every
Individual...

Renew by Phone
269-5222

_____

Renew on the Web
www.imcpl.org

For General Library Infomation
please call 275-4100